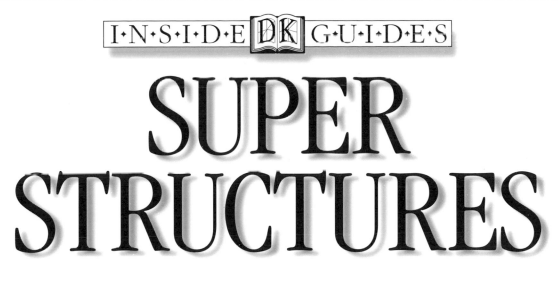

SUPER STRUCTURES

Written by

PHILIP WILKINSON

DORLING KINDERSLEY

London • New York • Stuttgart • Moscow

Pont de Normandie over the River
Seine near Honfleur, France

Semi-
submersible
service
vessel

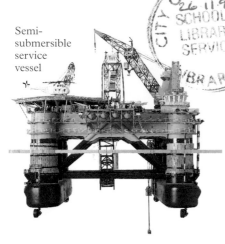

Headquarters of the Hongkong
and Shanghai Bank, Hong Kong

DK

A DORLING KINDERSLEY BOOK

Editor Laura Buller
Art editor Ann Cannings
Senior art editor Diane Klein
Managing editor Gillian Denton
Managing art editor Julia Harris
Editorial consultant David J. Brown
Research Julie Ferris
Additional design Diane Clouting
Picture research Jo Carlill
Production Charlotte Traill

Photography Andy Crawford, Geoff Brightling
Modelmakers Alec Saunders and the team at
Thorp Modelmakers; Chris Reynolds and the team at
BBC Visual Effects; Gerry Judah

First published in Great Britain in 1996
by Dorling Kindersley Limited,
9 Henrietta Street, Covent Garden, London WC2E 8PS

Copyright © 1996 Dorling Kindersley Limited, London
Visit us on the World Wide Web at http://www.dk.com

A CIP catalogue for this book is available from the
British Library.

ISBN 0 7513 5435X

Reproduced in Italy by G.R.B. Graphica, Verona
Printed in Singapore by Toppan

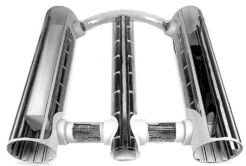

Triple tubes of the Channel
Tunnel, viewed from above

Murchison
oil platform
in the
North Sea

Triple-looped
roller coaster

Northbound, southbound, and
service tunnels, Channel Tunnel

Contents

Steam generator
inside a nuclear
reactor

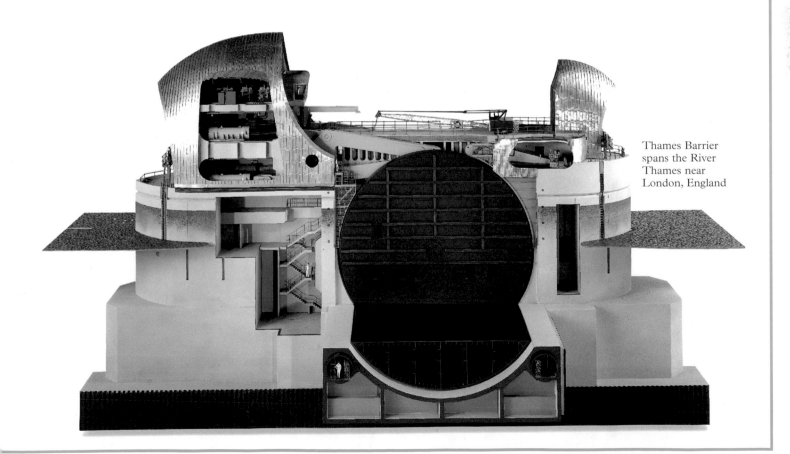

Thames Barrier
spans the River
Thames near
London, England

Building a super structure

Look inside some of the world's most amazing buildings and other permanent structures in the pages of this book. All of them have involved huge technological challenges – from designing a skyscraper able to withstand typhoon winds, to ensuring safety in a tunnel under the sea. Hundreds of people were involved in the building of each structure. Architects and engineers create the designs, draw up the plans, and build models that show what the structure will look like, how it will be built – and just how it works. Some of these models are featured in the following pages. During construction, teams of specialists work on different parts of the structure, from driving foundation piles deep into the soil to fitting the cables of a bridge.

Drawing office
In this 19th-century architect's office, draftsmen sit on high stools, crouching over their drawings. Today, architects and civil engineers are more likely to sit in front of computer screens to draw up their building plans.

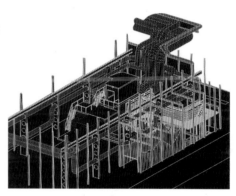

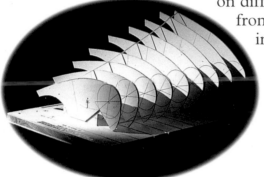

Working model
Many architects and engineers use models to help them work out the shape of a building and its individual parts. This simple wood and cardboard model was made to help design the curving roof shape of the main terminal building at Japan's Kansai Airport (pp. 32-33).

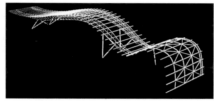

Computer model
Computer programs called CAD (computer-aided design) are useful tools for working out the details of complex structures, like the terminal roof at Kansai. CAD makes it easy to draw repeating elements, and to see the effects of changes quickly.

Invisible parts
Detailed drawings are made of parts of a structure that will be hidden away when it is finished. Most buildings, such as this scientific laboratory, have services such as cables and ventilation ducts hidden within the floors and walls. CAD is used to work out where everything will go.

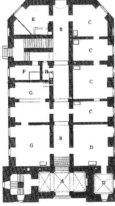

3-D model
A three-dimensional model of a structure and its site, like this one of the Inland Revenue Centre at Nottingham, England, is often used to show how the building will look in its local surroundings.

Shallow blocks
The separate blocks of this building are quite shallow in plan, allowing natural light to reach all the offices.

Floor plan
Architects use floor plans like this one to give precise information about the sizes of rooms, and the location of windows, doors, lifts, and staircases. Floor plans can also show details from the positions of electrical sockets to the building materials.

City within a city

The Inland Revenue Centre, designed by Michael Hopkins and Partners, is laid out in a series of blocks, to reflect the pattern of neighbouring city streets. The offices do not have air conditioning; instead, the structure itself is designed to keep air moving.

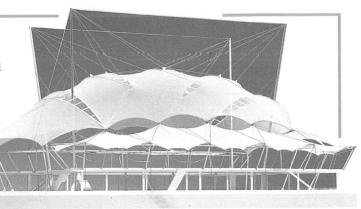

Sports hall

The Inland Revenue Centre has its own sports hall, with a tent-like fabric roof supported on steel poles. This model helped the architect and engineers to plan and test its design.

Natural ventilation

This model of the Inland Revenue Centre was made to show how its built-in ventilation system works.

Air outlets
The warm, stale air leaves the building through outlets at the top of the tower.

Stair tower
Warm air rises up the glazed towers on the corner of each block.

Hot air
Sunlight heats up the air in the stair towers, making it rise.

Soffits
These reflect less dazzling light back into the offices.

Light shelf
This shades the area near the windows and reflects light up to the soffits (undersides of the arches).

Opening windows
Fresh air enters the building through open windows.

Vents
Floor-level vents also act as fresh-air intakes.

Skyscraper

Soaring towers of steel, glass, and concrete, skyscrapers are the ultimate super structures. A skyscraper is a tall building in which the main weight of the structure is supported by a lightweight, strong framework, rather than by outside walls. In many skyscrapers the framework is hidden away inside, and the outside covered with a skin of lightweight material. This is why some office blocks look as if they are made of glass. But in the famous headquarters of the Hongkong Bank, the skeleton of steel columns and beams that holds the skyscraper together is visible on the outside.

Cross braces
Pairs of masts are connected by two-storey-high cross braces, which give the structure extra strength.

Suspension trusses
Like giant coat hangers, pairs of suspension trusses join the masts to support the hangers.

Hangers support floor beams

Masts
Arranged in two rows of four, each mast is made of four columns of tubular steel, linked by horizontal beams.

Floor beam

Column braced by short steel beams

Hanging together
The structure of the bank is based on eight tall masts which are made up of a cluster of steel tubes, joined by a series of rectangular beams like the rungs of a ladder. Huge diagonal beams, called trusses, connect the masts at five levels. Vertical steel hanger beams run down from each truss. The skyscraper's 44 main floors are hung from these beams.

Thinner at the top
The outer masts are shorter than the central pairs. This allows the building to "step back" at the top, so that it does not overshadow the street.

Chicago fire
After a devastating fire in 1871, the city centre of Chicago in the United States had to be rebuilt. Rising land prices made it cheaper to build up than out. So architects hit on the idea of designing tall buildings in which the weight was supported by a metal framework – the first skyscrapers.

Cladding
The steel used on the outside of the building is covered in a close-fitting aluminium cladding, to give a smooth and protective finish.

Double floors
Behind each huge truss is a double-height office floor.

Stairs
Glass-encased staircases run the full height of the building.

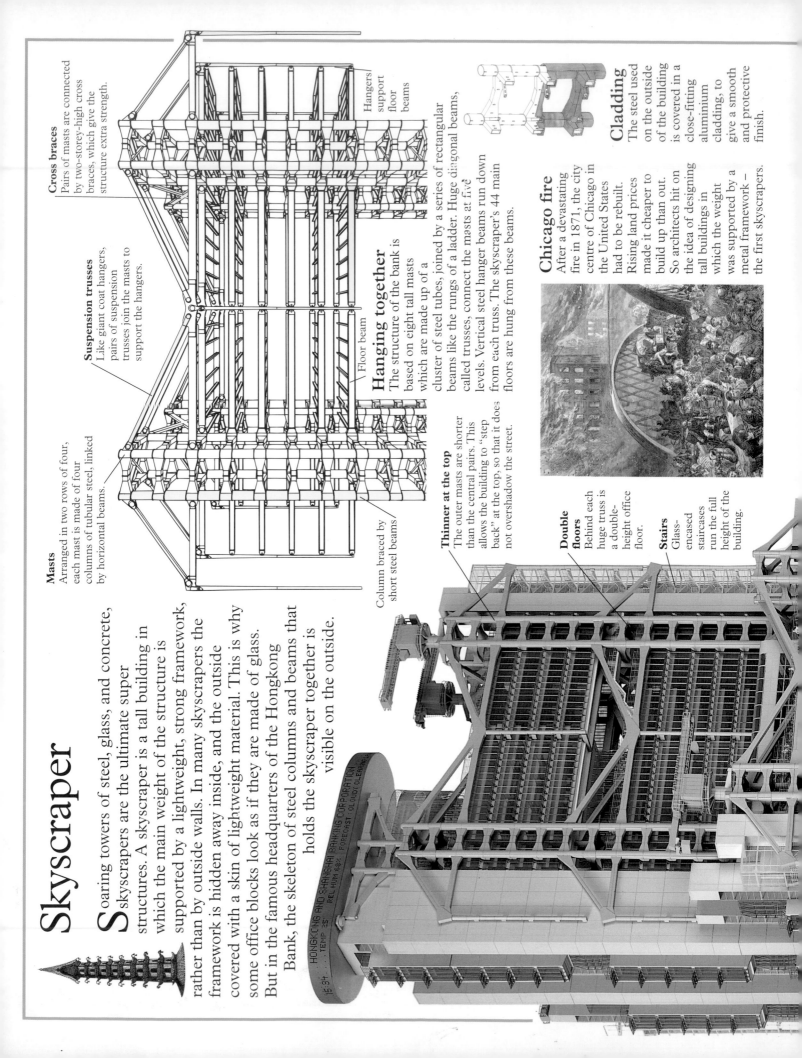

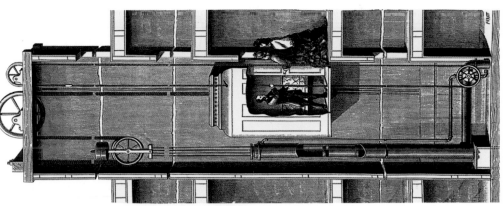

Continued on following page

Going up...

Tall buildings were not practical if you had to climb thousands of stairs to get to the top. Simple hoists had been around for centuries, but they were not safe for carrying people – if the cable broke, you could plummet to your death. In 1852 American engineer Elisha Graves Otis came up with a solution – the safety elevator. He developed a ratchet mechanism that "caught" the elevator if the cable broke.

Dangerous work

Many of the great American skyscrapers were built in the 1930s, before the introduction of modern safety precautions. Workers, nicknamed "skyboys", had little protection on scaffolding hundreds of metres high.

Catching the sun
The external sunscoop reflects natural light into the atrium.

The Hongkong Bank

Rising 46 storeys above Hong Kong island, the headquarters of the Hongkong Bank is one of the most innovative skyscrapers in the world. This building was designed by British architect Sir Norman Foster and completed in 1985. Its unusual external structure was designed by engineers Ove Arup and Partners.

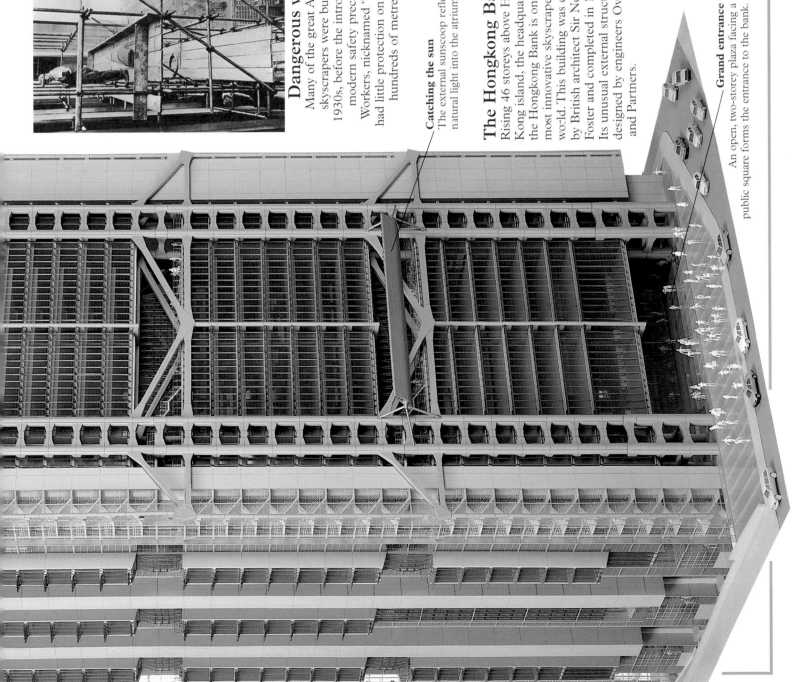

Grand entrance
An open, two-storey plaza facing a public square forms the entrance to the bank.

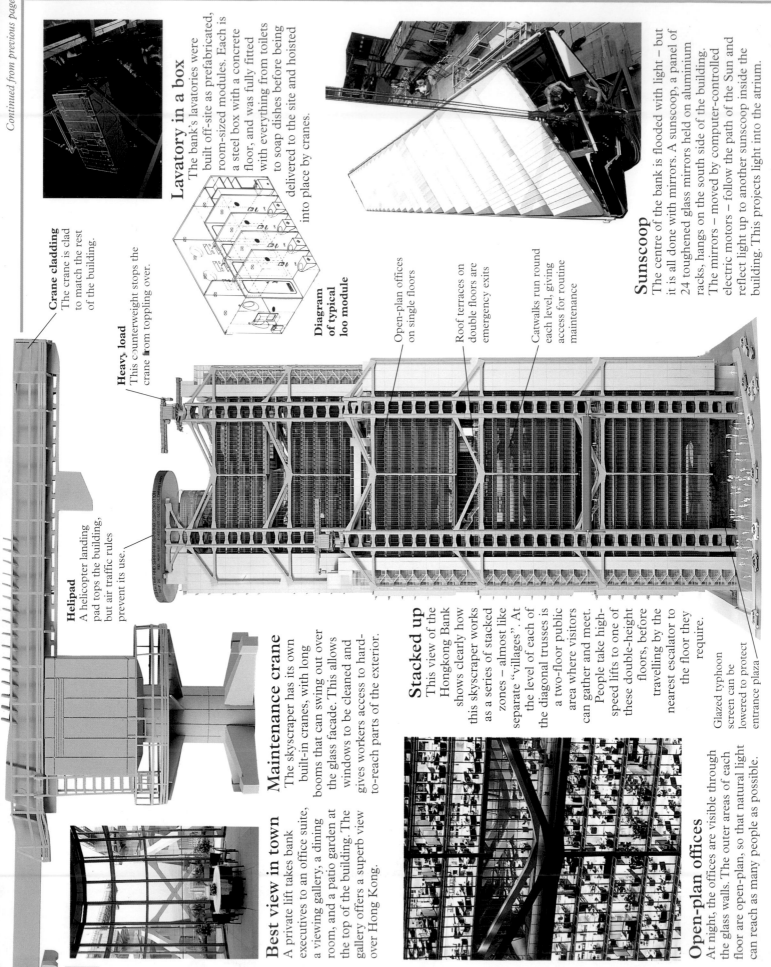

Lavatory in a box
The bank's lavatories were built off-site as prefabricated, room-sized modules. Each is a steel box with a concrete floor, and was fully fitted with everything from toilets to soap dishes before being delivered to the site and hoisted into place by cranes.

Diagram of typical loo module

Sunscoop
The centre of the bank is flooded with light – but it is all done with mirrors. A sunscoop, a panel of 24 toughened glass mirrors held on aluminium racks, hangs on the south side of the building. The mirrors – moved by computer-controlled electric motors – follow the path of the Sun and reflect light up to another sunscoop inside the building. This projects light into the atrium.

Crane cladding
The crane is clad to match the rest of the building.

Heavy load
This counterweight stops the crane from toppling over.

Helipad
A helicopter landing pad tops the building, but air traffic rules prevent its use.

Open-plan offices on single floors

Roof terraces on double floors are emergency exits

Catwalks run round each level, giving access for routine maintenance

Maintenance crane
The skyscraper has its own built-in cranes, with long booms that can swing out over the glass facade. This allows windows to be cleaned and gives workers access to hard-to-reach parts of the exterior.

Best view in town
A private lift takes bank executives to an office suite, a viewing gallery, a dining room, and a patio garden at the top of the building. The gallery offers a superb view over Hong Kong.

Stacked up
This view of the Hongkong Bank shows clearly how this skyscraper works as a series of stacked zones – almost like separate "villages". At the level of each of the diagonal trusses is a two-floor public area where visitors can gather and meet. People take high-speed lifts to one of these double-height floors, before travelling by the nearest escalator to the floor they require.

Glazed typhoon screen can be lowered to protect entrance plaza

Open-plan offices
At night, the offices are visible through the glass walls. The outer areas of each floor are open-plan, so that natural light can reach as many people as possible.

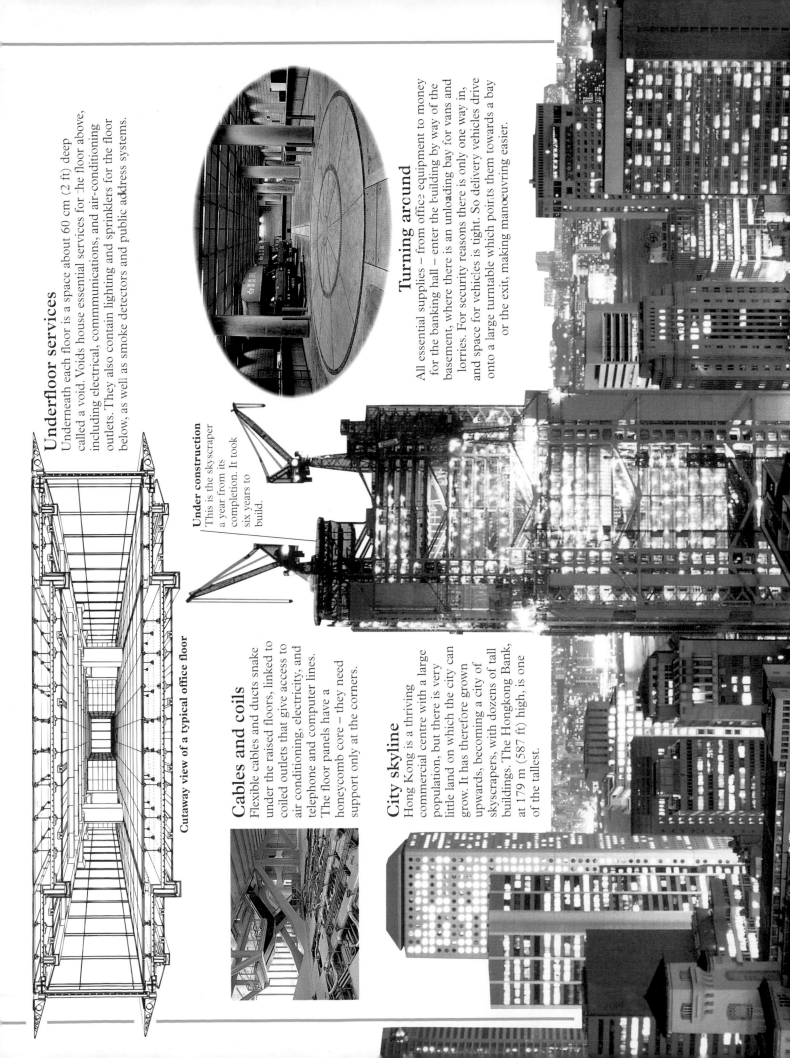

Underfloor services

Underneath each floor is a space about 60 cm (2 ft) deep called a void. Voids house essential services for the floor above, including electrical, communications, and air-conditioning outlets. They also contain lighting and sprinklers for the floor below, as well as smoke detectors and public address systems.

Under construction
This is the skyscraper a year from its completion. It took six years to build.

Cutaway view of a typical office floor

Cables and coils

Flexible cables and ducts snake under the raised floors, linked to coiled outlets that give access to air conditioning, electricity, and telephone and computer lines. The floor panels have a honeycomb core – they need support only at the corners.

City skyline

Hong Kong is a thriving commercial centre with a large population, but there is very little land on which the city can grow. It has therefore grown upwards, becoming a city of skyscrapers, with dozens of tall buildings. The Hongkong Bank, at 179 m (587 ft) high, is one of the tallest.

Turning around

All essential supplies – from office equipment to money for the banking hall – enter the building by way of the basement, where there is an unloading bay for vans and lorries. For security reasons there is only one way in, and space for vehicles is tight. So delivery vehicles drive onto a large turntable which points them towards a bay or the exit, making manoeuvring easier.

On stage

From theatre to ballet, opera to rock concerts, comedy to cabaret – the list of entertainments on offer in a modern city seems almost endless. But most cities cannot afford a separate building for each kind of event. The authorities in Cerritos, California met this challenge by creating a structure that is five buildings in one. The Cerritos Center for the Performing Arts, designed by Barton Myers Associates, uses modern technology to move almost 0.5 million kg (1 million lbs) of stage equipment – seats, floors, and ceilings – so that the interior of the auditorium can change according to the type of entertainment on offer, providing the audience with an exciting, ever-changing venue.

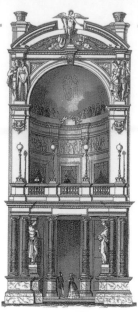

One building, one purpose
Traditional theatres are not very adaptable, because the floors, stage, and seating are usually fixed in place. Some Renaissance theatres of the 16th century even had permanent scenery.

Seating towers
Movable, steel-framed seating towers line the side walls.

Layered seats
Tiers of seats ensure that everyone in the audience has a good view of the stage.

Pivots
These allow the side seating towers to rotate inwards, away from the walls.

View from the stage
In this view, the theatre is arranged for drama. Behind the floor seating are three semi-circular tiers of seats. Towers hold boxes on both sides of the theatre.

On top
Flagpoles hung with bright banners top the roofs.

Entrance front
The Cerritos Center is highly decorated on the outside, with glass-enclosed lifts, hanging banners, and colourful geometric tilework. The walls are a mixture of polished red granite banded with limestone. Pyramid-shaped roofs top the towers and major sections of the arts complex.

Five theatre floor plans viewed from above

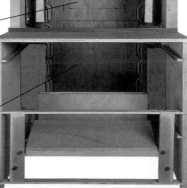

Raising the floor
Sunken panels lift to level the floor space.

Seat stores
Seats are stored under the floor.

Cabaret
For banquets and cabaret performances the entire floor is levelled to provide a large area for dining tables and chairs. The boxes are used for additional seating.

Swinging seats
The towers move inward on air-filled castors that glide across the floor.

Fly tower for scenery

Stage
The wide, deep stage is ideal for operas and musicals with large casts.

Lyric
A 1,450-seat opera house can be created by sliding some of the seating towers behind the stage, and lowering part of the floor to make an orchestra pit.

Take a seat

All but the tiered seats move so that everyone in the theatre has an excellent view of the performance. The towers contain small balconies that seat groups of eight or ten people.

Entrance lobby

The lobby is a spacious concrete structure joined to the auditorium at the tiered seating end. It provides access to each seating level, and plenty of room for the audience to circulate before shows and during intervals.

View from the circle

The arena arrangement allows for seating all around the auditorium. The seats closest to the stage are moved into place on air castors.

Rear-stage seats
This seating unit weighs 102,060 kg (225,000 lb), yet it can be moved away on air castors when not in use.

Podium
Four lifts can raise or lower sections of the floor to provide a raised podium – or a flat surface.

Side stage seating units
Two of these seating units, each weighing 63,504 kg (140,000 lb), flank the central stage.

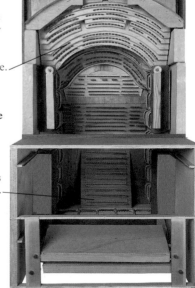

Angled arms
Tilting the arms brings the audience closer to the performers on stage.

Centre stage
The stage is in the middle, surrounded by seating.

Stay seated
Seats in the tiered levels are the only ones in the theatre that do not move.

Backstage seating
A raised platform behind the stage holds more seats.

Drama

Moving the stage forward from the lyric arrangement creates a more compact, 900-seat theatre. This is the right size for smaller-scale theatrical productions.

Arena

A raised podium stage and space enough for an audience of up to 1,780 people makes the arena arrangement ideal for sports events and rock concerts.

Concert

With a narrow central podium for the performers and seating boxes lining the walls, this arrangement provides a total of 1,936 seats – perfect for classical music concerts.

Big blue

With its vivid blue walls echoing the colours of the Mediterranean sea and sky, the regional government headquarters of Marseille, France is both a landmark and a symbol of the town. British architect William Alsop won a competition to design the building, known as *Le Grand Bleu* – the big blue. Its strong colour and unusual shapes make a lasting impression, but it is also a functional design which reflects the structure's two main uses – one building for the council chambers and another for administration offices. Its design also meets the challenges of the local weather – the strong winds that can cause damaging stresses on a building's structure and the dazzling southern sun.

Inside the atrium
The central space, or atrium, is open to the public. It provides access to a restaurant, crèche, library, information desk, and to the offices themselves. At one end is the ovoid, a steel-framed, oval-shaped pod used for exhibitions.

Unpeeled
The skin of the building is pulled back to expose the rib-like frame.

Walkways
The council building is wrapped with walkways.

Blue roof
A snake-like skin of blue triangular panels covers the council building roof.

What's inside?
Two council debating chambers, a function room, and a club are housed inside the council building.

Three into one
This view shows the building's three main parts: the curved aerofoil structure sits on top of the tall administration building, with the tapering oval of the council building seen in front. A stretched fabric awning covers much of the council building roof. This covering acts as a sun screen and also channels strong prevailing winds over the building.

In the shade
The walkway is shaded by the awning.

Steel rings of frame

Awning anchors
These rods anchor the roof awning.

The council building
This building stands on seven pairs of splayed concrete legs, which lift it above ground level. The legs support a rib-like framework of tubular steel rings, which are larger in the centre and smaller at the ends, giving the building its distinctive curve.

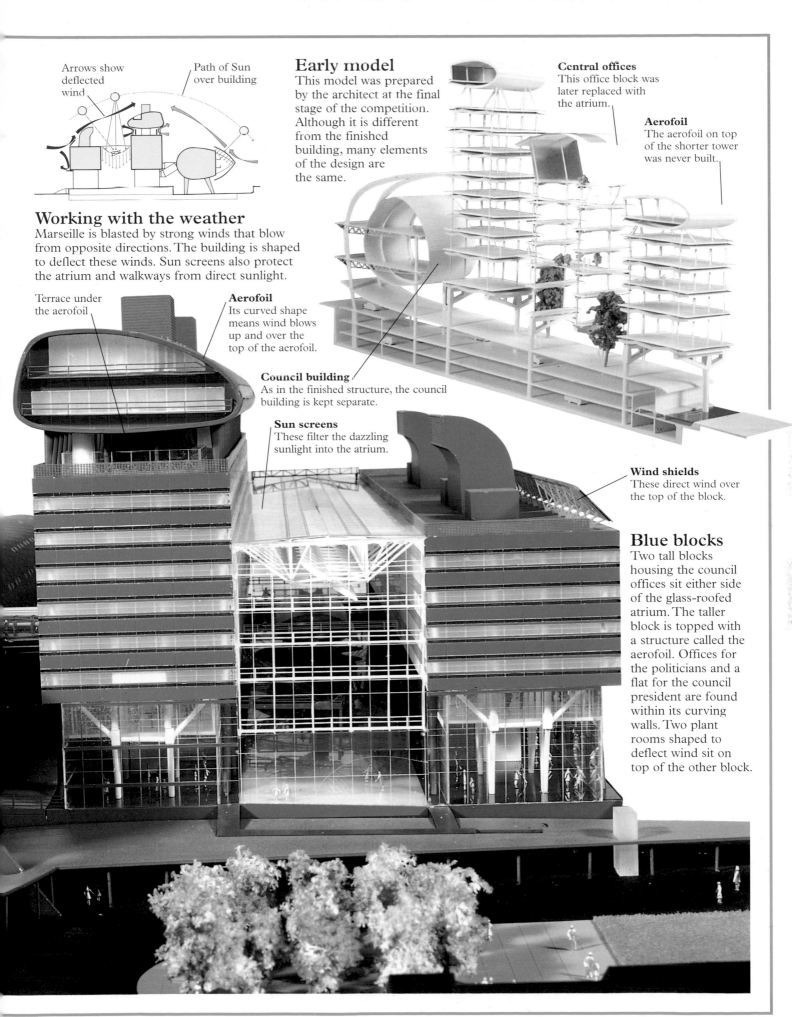

Arrows show deflected wind

Path of Sun over building

Early model

This model was prepared by the architect at the final stage of the competition. Although it is different from the finished building, many elements of the design are the same.

Central offices
This office block was later replaced with the atrium.

Aerofoil
The aerofoil on top of the shorter tower was never built.

Working with the weather

Marseille is blasted by strong winds that blow from opposite directions. The building is shaped to deflect these winds. Sun screens also protect the atrium and walkways from direct sunlight.

Terrace under the aerofoil

Aerofoil
Its curved shape means wind blows up and over the top of the aerofoil.

Council building
As in the finished structure, the council building is kept separate.

Sun screens
These filter the dazzling sunlight into the atrium.

Wind shields
These direct wind over the top of the block.

Blue blocks

Two tall blocks housing the council offices sit either side of the glass-roofed atrium. The taller block is topped with a structure called the aerofoil. Offices for the politicians and a flat for the council president are found within its curving walls. Two plant rooms shaped to deflect wind sit on top of the other block.

Beneath the streets

The veins and arteries of a modern city lie beneath its streets. Cables and pipes carry essential services like electricity and gas; drains take away waste; underground trains rush through tunnels. In most cities, the spate of excavating and tunnelling that provided all these services began in the 19th century, with hand-dug sewers. Many modern cables and pipes are still installed by hand, but engineers also use huge tunnel-boring machines. Early pipes were made of clay or iron, but these are being replaced by longer-lasting concrete and plastic, which can be colour-coded according to their contents. New technologies provide a need for new underground networks. One of the most recent is fibre optic cable, which can carry all kinds of information, from television and telephone signals to computer data.

City of the dead
The ancient Romans sometimes buried their dead in vast networks of underground passages called catacombs. These, at Tyre, Lebanon, date from 200 AD. The remains of the deceased were placed on shelves or their ashes were deposited in urns after cremation.

Road surface of crushed rock mixed with bitumen and sand

Mixed rocks such as limestone and granite make the road base

Subsoil

The first sewers
Raw sewage once poured through open ditches. As cities grew, the sight and smell became so bad that vast sewage pipes were built. The first were dug by hand and lined with arching brick vaults. Many of these are still in use.

Slice through a city
Each section of this model shows one slice beneath a typical city street. Just below pavement level are the essential services from drains to telephone lines needed by every house in the street. Lower down are the underground trains and the main sewers that serve large numbers of homes. Deep water supply tunnels are found at the lowest level, far beneath the surface.

Pumping water
Water is supplied to large cities through vast concrete tunnels. These can be up to 2.5 m (8 ft) wide – big enough to drive a car through. The water is brought to the surface by huge electric pumps like these, housed underground.

Twin tunnels
Concrete-lined tunnels carry water from treatment plants to supply the entire city.

Network of sewers
carries waste into
large main
sewer

Electric street
lighting

Water from
street runs
through
drains into
sewer

Each pair of
wires in a
telephone cable
carries one call

Fresh water
supply

Computerised pig

Pipelines must be kept in good repair, but it is
difficult to check a pipe for flaws once it is buried.
Engineers send remote-controlled inspection units,
nicknamed "pigs" due to their long, rounded
shape, down pipelines, to check them from the
inside. Sensors around the pig spot defects and
send data to a built-in
computer. The data is read
when the pig finishes its run.

Cable for television
and radio signals

Gas pipes have thick
walls to prevent leaks

Low-voltage
electricity cable

High-voltage
electricity cable

Modern
main sewer
lined with
concrete
rings

Safe under the streets

During World War II, German
planes bombarded British cities
at night in a campaign called the
Blitz. Thousands of people
sheltered, and even slept, on the
station platforms of London's
underground railway. When an
air-raid warning sounded, people
ran down into the nearest station.

Tube tunnels
Underground
trains run in deep
tunnels excavated
beneath building
foundations.

Tunnels under the sea

Linking Britain with the rest of Europe for the first time since people crossed the frozen wastes during the last Ice Age, the Channel Tunnel is a spectacular engineering feat. The 50.5 km (31 miles) triple-tubed tunnel, of which 38 km (23 miles) are under the sea, took less than seven years to build. Enormous tunnel boring machines pushed their way through about 7 million cu m (247 million cu ft) of rock, leaving completed sections of tunnel behind. Although the underwater tunnels are the heart of the system, the project also included three land tunnels, two terminals, and passenger, car shuttle, and freight trains.

Eurostar trains

Passengers without cars travel through the tunnel on high-speed Eurostar trains. Based on the design of the French TGV, the trains reach a maximum speed of 300 km/h (186 mph) – 160 km/h (100 mph) in the tunnel itself. A journey from London to Paris takes three hours; Brussels takes 15 minutes more.

Tunnel dreams

People have dreamed and schemed about a tunnel under the Channel for hundreds of years. This 1914 drawing shows one fanciful idea of how the tunnel might work.

Dumping ground

Much of the chalky rock dug from the tunnel ended up in this huge reservoir at Fond Pignon, France. Mixed with water into a yogurt-like slurry and pumped into the reservoir, the tunnel spoil set hard in a layer 40 m (131 ft) thick.

Emergency services

Specially built vehicles, kitted out as fire engines, ambulances, or maintenance units, speed along the central service tunnel in an emergency. They can reach any part of the tunnel in 20 minutes.

Inside the tunnels

Each of the tunnels is packed with equipment – drainage, cooling, and ventilation systems, electrical power supplies for the trains, lighting, computerised control systems, and railway tracks. Equipment for looking after all these systems is contained in the cross-passages and in the service vehicles which travel along the central tunnel.

A slice through the tunnel
The model shown below and on the next page shows a typical cross-section through the three underwater tunnels.

Electric cables

Drainage pipes

Firefighting equipment

Electricity supply
Some 1,300 km (808 miles) of electrical cable run along the tunnels, carrying power for lighting, signals, ventilation equipment, and the trains themselves.

Guidance system
Wires buried beneath the service tunnel floor guide the maintenance vehicles. The vehicles pick up signals from the wires, so that they can be steered automatically.

Cooling water pipes

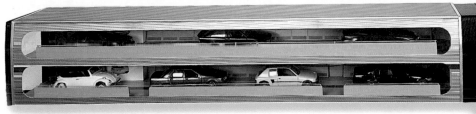

Le Shuttle trains

Passengers with cars travel under the Channel on Le Shuttle. These trains are made up of 28 transporter wagons which can carry up to five cars on each of their twin decks. Passengers can sit in their cars or stand in the wagons during the 30-minute journey. There are also special wagons for larger vehicles.

Three-in-one

The Channel Tunnel really consists of three separate tunnels, two for trains and a central service tunnel for maintenance and for use in emergencies. The three tunnels are connected every 375 m (1,230 ft) by cross-passages, which can be sealed off with massive metal bulkhead doors in case of fire.

Relief duct
These ducts loop over the service tunnel to link the two running tunnels every 250 m (820 ft). When a train speeds through the tunnel, it creates high air pressure ahead of it. The ducts relieve this pressure by allowing air to escape into the other running tunnel.

Running tunnel
Trains speed through the twin running tunnels. These are lined with the strongest concrete ever made. More than 470,000 precast concrete rings, reinforced with a metal cage, form the watertight lining.

Service tunnel
The first of the three underwater tunnels to be finished was the service tunnel. Its excavation helped engineers to overcome any problems on a small scale before boring the two larger running tunnels.

Cross passages
These links between all three tunnels house emergency and maintenance equipment and carry fresh pressurized air to the running tunnels.

Le Shuttle train

Drainage pipes

Eurostar train

Cooling pipes
Chilled water runs through these pipes to take away excess heat given off by trains.

Main lighting

Piston relief duct

Communication cables
Many of the cables in the service tunnels carry information – train signals, telephone lines, and fibre optic cables for computer data.

Tunnel trackwork
Nearly 200 km (124 miles) of track, with 174 points and crossings and turnaround loops at each end, form the tunnel railway.

Continued on following page

21

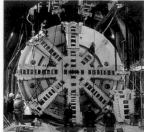

Cutting head

At the end of each tunnel boring machine (TBM) is an 800-tonne rotating cutting head (above), tipped with tough tungsten carbide picks for drilling rock.

Cutting head
The head rotates as it pushes through the rock.

Operator's control cabin

Gripper shoes
These grip the rock and thrust the TBM forwards.

Tailskin and shutter

Digging under the sea

The Channel Tunnel was cut with eleven giant TBMs. This is a model of one TBM and its back-up services. Because it is so long, the TBM is shown from left to right, over four rows.

Crane
Lining segments are lifted with this crane and placed on a conveyer belt for delivery to the erectors.

Right track
Supply trains run along narrow-gauge railway tracks right through the TBM back-up.

Ups and downs
Ladders connect each of the gantries of the TBM.

Adjustable belt
The conveyer can be extended to reach the right spoil wagon.

Spoil wagons
These wagons carry the excavated rock back to the tunnel entrance.

Conveyer discharge
The spoil pours off the conveyer belt into waiting wagons.

Meals on wheels
A canteen car – as well as an office, workshop, and toilets – moves along with the TBM.

Ventilation duct
Fresh air is taken in through the main ventilation duct for circulation to the tunnel face.

Passenger car
The tunnel operators travelled to work on this train. Three shifts of 21 men worked round the clock.

Providing a push
This locomotive powers the supply train. Most trains were several hundred metres long.

Tunnel lining segments
The curved concrete rings that line the tunnel were pushed into place by machines called erectors.

Spoil removal
Some 11,000 cu m (388,410 cu ft) of excavated rock, or spoil, had to be removed each week.

Spare segments
There is storage space within the TBM back-up for extra concrete tunnel lining segments.

Conveyer belts
This conveyer belt moves lining segments to the tunnel face, while the lower belt takes away spoil.

Air supply
Ducts deliver a constant supply of fresh air to the tunnel face.

Grouting equipment
Gaps between the lining segments were filled with grout, kept here.

Power pack
Electricity to run the TBM is provided by power packs.

Gantries
The levels of the TBM and its back-up are known as gantries.

Wrong track
When the tunnel was finished, the narrow supply train track was replaced with full-sized track.

Removing the rock
Every supply train carried nine spoil wagons – each able to take away 14 cu m (494 cu ft) of rock.

Power supply
Transformers ensured that the electricity supplied to the power packs was of the correct voltage.

Dust removal
Because the spoil was so dry and dusty, huge fans were used to keep the machinery dust-free.

Extending pipes
As the tunnel grew, pipes carrying air, water, and electric cables were also extended.

Duct trailers
These trailers at the end of the TBM back-up carry giant reels of spare ducting.

Underground breakthrough
Each tunnel was bored by two TBMs, one starting in France, the other in England. Eventually the two teams met in the middle, over 100 m (320 ft) under the sea. Each time this happened, there was a celebration.

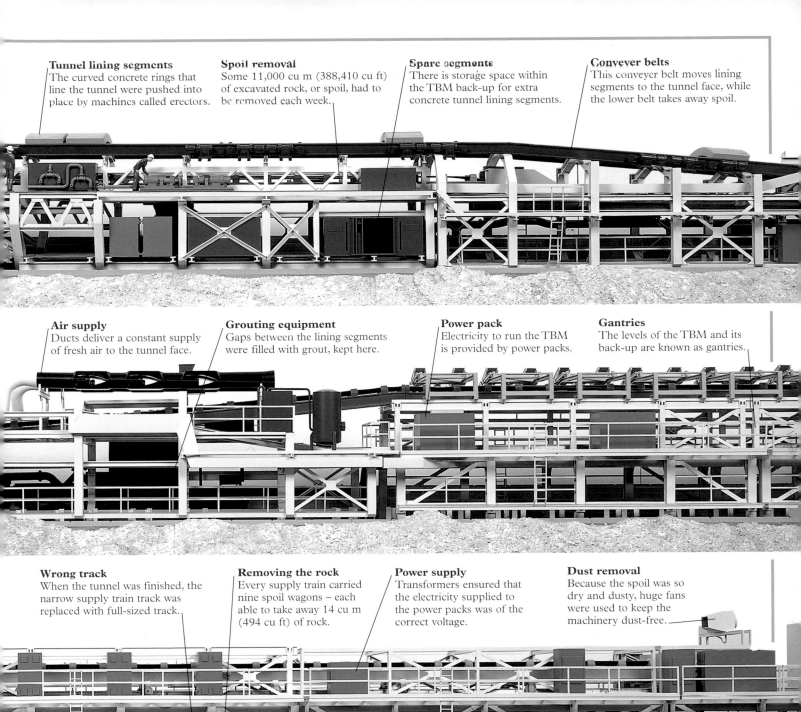

Grand span

Since our prehistoric ancestors threw a log across a stream to get from one side to the other, people have built bridges. Several types of bridge have emerged, from the elegant arched bridges of the Romans, to the beautiful suspension bridges of the 19th and 20th centuries. A bridge must be strong enough to support its own weight as well as the weight of the vehicles crossing it. The difference between the main types of bridge is the way the forces exerted by the bridge's weight are displaced. Bridges must also work with the forces of nature, from strong winds and freezing temperatures to storms and earthquakes. France's Pont de Normandie, featured on the following pages, meets all these demands.

Beam bridge

The first bridge was probably a simple beam bridge, made by putting a plank across a stream. To span a wider distance, piers could be built up from the river bed to support a few beams, end to end. Some ancient stone beam bridges still survive, like this one in Dartmoor, England. Both its piers and beams are made of hard, long-lasting granite.

Built to last

The world's first iron bridge was built across the River Severn at Coalbrookdale, England, in 1779. The town already had a booming iron industry – the first cast-iron railway lines were made there – so iron, with its high tensile strength, was an obvious choice for the bridge. Most bridges built in the next century had spans of cast or wrought iron.

A deadly collapse

This rail bridge over the River Tay in Scotland, built in 1878, was an impressive structure some 3.2 km (2 miles) long, but the girders of the central spans were not securely joined to the others. The bridge collapsed during a gale on 29 December 1879, killing 75 passengers on a train crossing the bridge.

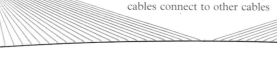

Cables connect directly to towering pylons; in a suspension bridge, most cables connect to other cables

Cable-stayed bridge

The Pont de Normandie is a cable-stayed bridge. In this type of design, cables bear the weight of the deck and transfer it to the pylons and the access viaducts on either side. This means that the loads of the central deck and access viaducts balance each other, similar to a person carrying a suitcase in each hand.

Roadway
Two lanes of traffic cross the bridge in each direction.

Arch bridge

This type of bridge is used to cross a span where it is difficult to build supporting piers. The arch transfers the downwards-pressing load into the ground at either end of the bridge.

Cantilever bridge

In this bridge, arms extend outwards from central supports. Because it can cross a long span and can be made stiff and strong, it is ideal for heavy loads.

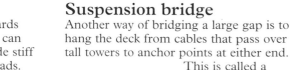

Suspension bridge

Another way of bridging a large gap is to hang the deck from cables that pass over tall towers to anchor points at either end. This is called a suspension bridge.

Forth Rail Bridge

This large cantilever bridge in Scotland was designed by Sir John Fowler and Benjamin Baker and finished in 1889. In all it is about 2.5 km (1.5 miles) long, with steel cantilevers supporting two main spans 46 m (151 ft) above the waters of the Firth of Forth. The total weight of steel in the bridge is some 58,000 tonnes.

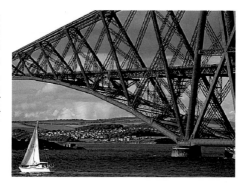

Tyne Bridge

One of several bridges over the River Tyne in Newcastle, England, this bridge is of a steel arch design, with the roadway suspended from the arch by a rigid network of steel girders. The towers at either end act as weights to hold down the outwards thrust of the arch.

Pylons
Each concrete pylon is shaped like an upside-down letter Y.

Mackinac Bridge

Though its central span is shorter than others, the very long side spans of the Mackinac suspension bridge in Michigan, United States made it overall the world's longest at 2.6 km (1.6 miles) when it opened in 1957.

Super span
From pylon to pylon, the central span is 856 m (2,808 ft) long.

Pylon anchors 23 pairs of cables

Across the waters
The Pont de Normandie crosses the estuary of the River Seine.

Nose lifter
A tower crane lifted away the temporary launching nose.

Pylon

Launching nose

Access spans
This sequence shows how the bridge was constructed. Access spans were built by installing each concrete deck section in turn from a temporary launching nose, a movable gantry.

Concrete cantilevers
The next stage was to add the concrete deck sections hung out from the main pylons. These were cast in position. Cables were added after each section was cast.

Cables

Balanced deck
The deck section is cantilevered, or balanced by one on the other side.

Balancing length of deck

Pier

Cables
The stay cables were replaced by final cables.

Balancing act
One by one, the remaining concrete sections were hung from each pylon. Stay cables supported each section until it was balanced by its partner.

Deck built out from pylon

Ready to hang
Once the access span was linked with the cantilevered sections, the steel decks that form the centre of the span were ready to hang.

Free end of span

Rigid deck
Concrete decks help make the bridge rigid.

Meeting in the middle
Each steel deck was shipped downriver on a barge, lifted by a moving crane installed on the last deck segment, and welded into place. In this way, the decks grew towards each other to meet in the middle.

Moving crane

Barge

Pont de Normandie
This stunning cable-stayed bridge, designed by M. Virlogeux, connects the French towns of Le Havre and Honfleur. It is 2,141 m (7,025 ft) long in total. Two types of deck form the bridge: concrete decks lead up to and stretch just beyond the pylons, while the centre part of the span is made of box-like steel sections.

Pylons
These tower some 200 m (656 ft) above their footings – two-thirds the height of the Eiffel Tower in Paris.

Rainwater ridges
Because trickling rainwater can make a bridge sway, the cable sheaths are ridged.

Stay cables
Made of up to 51 separate steel strands, the cables are covered in a plastic sheath. This keeps the strands together and protects them from the weather.

Built on piers
Leading up to each pylon are the approach spans. These are built on piers supported by piled foundations sunk 42 m (138 ft) into the riverbed.

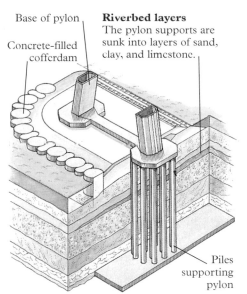

Base of pylon

Concrete-filled cofferdam

Riverbed layers
The pylon supports are sunk into layers of sand, clay, and limestone.

Piles supporting pylon

Protecting the pylon

Because the northern pylon of the bridge sits in the river, it had to be protected from collisions with ships. A ring of cofferdams made up of concrete-filled sheet piles surrounds the footings of the pylon.

Anchorage boxes
Cables are fixed to anchorage boxes on the upper sections of the pylons.

Damper cables

Bridge engineers had to ensure that the cables would not sway into each other in high winds. So damper cables, which hang at right angles to the main cables, were fitted to reduce possible movement.

Cable pairs
The cables are anchored in pairs, one on each side of the deck.

Lifting the deck into place

A mobile crane lifted each section of deck to within 50 cm (20 in) of its correct position, before it was eased into place and welded to its neighbours. Only then were this section's cables installed so that the crane could release its grip.

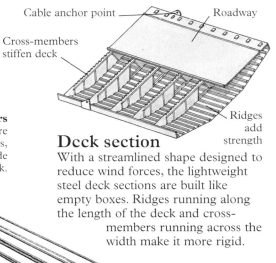

Cable anchor point

Roadway

Cross-members stiffen deck

Ridges add strength

Deck section

With a streamlined shape designed to reduce wind forces, the lightweight steel deck sections are built like empty boxes. Ridges running along the length of the deck and cross-members running across the width make it more rigid.

Taming the tides

Ever since the Romans founded Londinium on the banks of the River Thames, it has been prone to sudden flooding. As the city of London grew, the threat increased. The biggest menace comes from surge tides that can sweep across the North Sea, raising the sea level by 300 mm (1 ft) and pushing water up the Thames at speeds of up to 96 km/h (60 mph). After several disastrous floods earlier this century, the government decided to build a barrier across the river. The Thames Barrier consists of a series of gates, which can be opened to let ships pass, and closed when there is a chance of flooding.

A disastrous flood
In 1953, the Thames spilled over its banks east of London. More than 300 people lost their lives, damage to buildings cost millions of pounds, and 65,000 hectares (160,000 acres) of farmland were swamped by salt water.

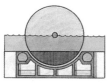

Open position

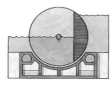

Flood control position

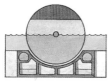

Maintenance position

Turning gates
Each of the Barrier's gates can close to form a wall five storeys high in just 20 minutes. The gates are raised to the top for maintenance.

Inside the Barrier
Under the curving pier roofs are the powerful hydraulic mechanisms that move the gates. Between the piers are the gates themselves. Those nearest the riverbanks are lifted above or lowered into the water. The gates in the centre can swing beneath the water when opened, so ships can pass above.

Rocking rams
A pair of hydraulic rams inside each pier push and pull to raise the rocking beam.

Steel shells
Each pier roof is a curving shell made of triple layered timber covered with a protective skin of stainless steel sheets.

Access tunnel
Linking the sills are two service tunnels, big enough for engineers to walk through. These carry power cables, control cables, and drains, and provide access to all parts of the Barrier.

Concrete cradle
The central gates are cradled in huge curving concrete sills. These massive structures – the largest weighs 10,000 tonnes – were built on the riverbank. Tugboats towed them out to the piers, where they were flooded and sunk to the riverbed so that the gates could be built onto them.

Cofferdams

Before the Barrier could be built, engineers had to construct cofferdams. These are submerged steel boxes, from which the water is pumped to provide a dry building site. They were made by driving piles up to 24 m (78 ft) into the riverbed. The piers were built on top of the cofferdams.

Gate arm
The gate arm rotates round a central shaft like a wheel on an axle. Each arm is loaded with steel to help counterbalance the weight of the gate. Wooden strips crisscross the arm, protecting it from impact by passing ships.

Central pier
Sunk some 16 m (52 ft) into the solid chalk riverbed, the central piers are 11 m (36 ft) wide and 65 m (213 ft) long. Navigation lights at each end tell ships whether the gates are open or shut.

Maintenance crane
Each pier is topped with a crane for machinery maintenance.

Rocker beams
Pairs of reversible hydraulic rams – one pulling and one pushing – move huge mechanical arms called rocker beams. The tips of the beams are connected to the gate arms, so that when the rocker beams move, the gate is lifted or lowered into position. This is quite a task – each gate weighs a massive 3,700 tonnes.

Shift and latch
When the gate has been moved to its required position it is vital that it is held there. The shift and latch mechanism acts like an enormous bolt, locking the gate closed so that the pressure of a surge tide cannot force it open.

Lift
A lift links the top of the pier with the service tunnel below.

Barrier gates
Plated with high-strength steel, the gates are made of hollow cells. They are protected from corrosion by 40 tonnes of paint.

Gap in the gate
A small space between the gate and sill lets some water through, to keep the river flowing.

Access tunnel

Sand ballast

Steel piles
These piles are the edge of the cofferdam, inside which the pier was built.

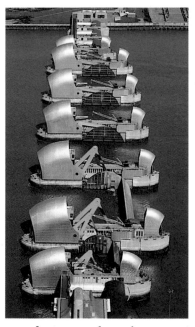

Across the river
From bank to bank, the Barrier is about 520 m (1,706 ft) wide. Each of its four central openings spans 61 m (200 ft) – wide enough for ships to pass. Weather conditions and tide levels are monitored at the Barrier control centre, enabling staff to decide when to close the gates. So far, the gates have been closed more than twenty times.

Loop the loop

$\mathbb{A}$fter an agonisingly slow haul to the top of a steep slope, a roller coaster is allowed to hurtle down the tracks, picking up speed as gravity pulls the cars downhill. As the coaster climbs to take the first loop, its riders feel sheer exhilaration. The coaster shoots upwards, apparently defying gravity to hang briefly in mid-air at the top of the loop. The cars roll down again – but there's another stomach-churning loop just ahead. This mixture of fear and anticipation is probably what makes roller coasters so popular at today's amusement parks. The engineer's job is to make sure the ride is terrifying – yet also perfectly safe. Modern coasters have many safety features built in, from strengthened supports for the framework to specially designed brakes for the cars.

Coaster disaster
Early roller coasters provided thrills – and spills. This engraving shows a man thrown to his death from a roller coaster car at Saint-Cloud, France in 1891. Modern coasters use padded steel safety bars that hinge over the shoulders of each passenger, pinning them in place until the end of the ride.

Heavy metal
The framework of a coaster this size contains about 2,500 tonnes of steel.

Momentum gained from the loops will push the coaster up the slope

Heels over heads
On the Nemesis ride at England's Alton Towers theme park, the cars are suspended from the track, leaving the riders' feet dangling in mid-air. The idea is to make the passengers feel even less secure than on a traditional roller coaster, although the design is quite safe.

Side braces for looping section of coaster

Tubes and ties
The coaster cars speed on air-filled tyres over their steel path. Its twin parallel tubes are secured to steel ties.

Wooden coaster
The first roller coasters were built of wood, and many new coasters are built in the same way. With its framework reinforced with cross-members, a wooden structure can be just as safe as a steel one, and enthusiasts claim that their slight flexing movement adds to the thrill of the ride.

Thick, tubular steel frame supports the rising track

Steel roller coaster
Modern steel roller coasters sometimes have one or more upside-down loops, as well as the steep up-and-down slopes of older coasters. This one turns its riders head over heels three times in all. It runs on a track made of steel tubes which reaches a height of almost 15 m (49 ft) at the tops of the loops. As they race around the track, the cars reach a top speed of about 100 km/h (60 mph).

Track attachment

Roller coaster cars run on wheels like railway carriages, but various safety devices stop them falling off the track, or rolling backwards down the hill if the chain mechanism fails. In this design, a second set of wheels can grip the track for added security.

Air-filled tyres for smooth ride

Pinned to the track
At the top of the loop, the cars are pushed against the track by centripetal force, which keeps a rotating object moving in a circle.

Steel safety bars keep riders in their seats

Steel framework

The tubular steel framework that supports the raised section of the roller coaster is strengthened with diagonal braces that cross between each upright and horizontal beam.

Steel tubes brace the structure from the side

Teardrop loop
The curve in a looping coaster is not a full circle, but a teardrop shape. This kind of loop creates more centripetal force at a slower speed, keeping passengers thrilled – but safe.

Colouring a coaster
It takes thousands of litres of paint to colour a coaster. A roller coaster of this size would need enough paint to cover more than five football pitches.

Strong supports
Thick steel tubes shaped like inverted letter Vs are sunk on deep foundations to provide firm support for the coaster track.

Super airport

Air travel brings the world closer together – jets carry people and cargo between its major cities in just a few hours. Its increasing popularity has led to a need for larger airports that can operate 24 hours a day. But a busy airport operating all night disturbs local people and pollutes the atmosphere. One amazing airport provides a solution: Kansai International Airport is built on its own artificial island, about 5 km (3 miles) away from the shore of Honshu, Japan's main island. The terminal had to be made strong enough – and flexible enough – to withstand earthquakes and typhoon winds, and large enough to accommodate some 25 million passengers a year. To meet these demands, architect Renzo Piano, with engineers Ove Arup and Partners, designed a vast building some 1,660 m (1 mile) long, with an elegant, curving roof.

An artificial island

Kansai stands on an artificial island, about 4.5 km (2.8 miles) long and 2.5 km (1.5 miles) wide, in Osaka Bay. The island was made by building a rectangular sea wall around the edge of the site and then filling the area in the middle. A six-lane highway, a railway, and high-speed ferries provide access to the island.

Roof trusses

Made of tubular steel, the passenger terminal's striking triangular roof trusses rest on splayed support legs. They are designed to be rigid under normal conditions, but are flexible enough to bend without breaking in the event of an earthquake. The white "sails" between the trusses are ventilation ducts that send fresh air through the terminal.

Cladding

The curving roof of the terminal building is clad, or covered, with stainless steel panels. These are designed to resist corrosion from salt and pollution in the air. The side walls are clad with large sheets of glass, so that the terminal is flooded with sunlight.

Floors for flights
Each floor of the terminal serves a different purpose, with domestic departures and arrivals sandwiched between the international floors.

Curving roof truss

Ins and outs
Passengers arrive at the terminal on the lower level and depart on the upper level.

Canyon
This four-storey reception area provides access to each level of the terminal.

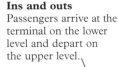

Under the roof

Beneath its cladding of 90,000 shiny steel panels, the structure of the terminal roof is clearly visible. Long rib-like trusses are connected by steel beams. These are attached to the pointed tops of the trusses every 4 m (13 ft) along their length.

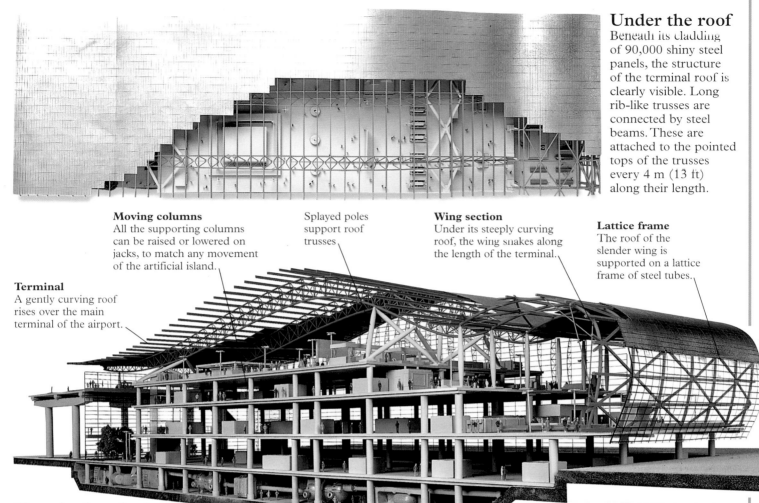

Moving columns
All the supporting columns can be raised or lowered on jacks, to match any movement of the artificial island.

Splayed poles support roof trusses.

Wing section
Under its steeply curving roof, the wing snakes along the length of the terminal.

Lattice frame
The roof of the slender wing is supported on a lattice frame of steel tubes.

Terminal
A gently curving roof rises over the main terminal of the airport.

Terminal and wing

The roof's double curve shows how the structure is divided into two parts. The main terminal contains the check-ins, customs area, baggage handling facilities, restaurants, and shops. The "wing" at one end houses the arrival and departure gates, next to which the aircraft park.

Travelling the world

After World War II, air travel became more common. Jet airliners like this Stratocruiser were developed that could cross the Atlantic in around 12 hours. Gradually, air travel became cheaper, and more and more large international airports were built.

Checkpoints
Security and passport checkpoints are on the top floor of the terminal.

Boarding
Passengers waiting at the boarding gates can see the runway through curving glass windows.

Basement
Machine rooms and building services are housed here.

Bridge
This links the gates with the waiting aircraft.

Floor by floor

A slice through the main terminal building shows how each of the four floors has its own function. On the "landside" of the terminal (far left), access roads bring buses and taxis right up to the terminal. On the "airside", boarding bridges connect the aircraft with the terminal.

Stacked up

Bangkok, Thailand is one of the most congested cities in the world – its population has doubled over the last 30 years. Because there is no underground railway, most people jump into their cars, creating terrible traffic jams. The railways run at ground level, and the level crossings also bring cars to a stop. The solution is to raise both trains and major roads above the ground. This is the idea behind BERTS – the Bangkok Elevated Road and Train System. On completion, BERTS will bring trains and vehicles 53 km (33 miles) from Rangsit in the north and Huamac in the east, into the centre of Bangkok. BERTS needed to be built quickly, over existing railway tracks, so the engineers, Ove Arup and Partners, designed concrete sections that were cast off-site and assembled at speed.

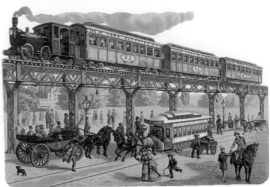

Raising the railway
The idea of running a railway on overhead tracks to ease street congestion is an old one. Many early city railways, like this line built in New York City in the 1880s, were raised up on tall viaducts to clear obstructions below. People – and horse-drawn carriages – could pass through the spaces underneath.

Shops and offices
Raising the roads and rails creates space for shops and offices beneath. There are also plans to develop hotels and offices at major stations.

Six-lane highway
The elevated highway on top of BERTS has three lanes in each direction to ease traffic congestion.

Windows
Cut into the concrete walls, window openings provide ventilation for the railway – and a view of the city.

Lifting the load
Concrete pillars hold up the elevated sections. These are supported by piles sunk up to 50 m (164 ft) deep.

Strong concrete pillars

Saving space and time
BERTS saves space by cramming two railways, a highway, shops, and stations onto what was once trackside land forming the old state railway into the city centre. To save construction time, BERTS is built from precast concrete boxes. Each weighs 1,500 tonnes and is wide enough for two railway tracks, or one track and a station platform.

High highways

Most modern motorways have elevated sections and approach roads raised on columns. When two roads meet, this creates a complex pattern of roads on different levels, seen here in Atlanta, United States.

Gridlock

When Bangkok's traffic grinds to a halt, people have little choice but to turn off their car engines and wait – or get out and walk. The city's traffic planners hope that BERTS will ease congestion and cut travel times.

State railway This network connects Bangkok with cities throughout Thailand.

Local railway Three million people a day will use the community trains.

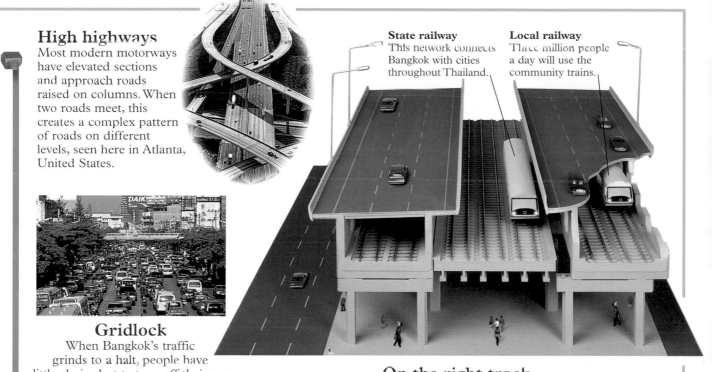

On the right track

The triple tracks of the state railway run in the centre of the structure, while community trains travel along each side. At street level, local roads will travel beside the elevated system, giving access to the elevated highway and the shops and offices.

Shops at street level

Atom power

A t the heart of a nuclear reactor like Sizewell B, tiny atoms of uranium are split to unleash a force that approaches the heat and light of the Sun – and to turn on ten million light bulbs. Nuclear power stations capture this heat to boil water into jets of steam, which drive huge turbines to produce electricity. Because the power of a nuclear reaction is so great – and potentially so dangerous – it has to take place in an incredibly strong container, called a pressure vessel. This is housed in a vast domed tower of concrete and steel, designed to keep in any radioactive material in the event of a leak, and to withstand external dangers, from an earthquake to a plane crash.

Sizewell site

This aerial view shows the complex of buildings that make up the power station – everything from turbine houses to fuel stores and workshops. The power station is close to the coast because cold sea water is used to cool down the exhaust steam from the turbines, turning it back to water before it is pumped back to the steam generator to be re-used.

Safety suits

There are no workers in the containment building – because the high radiation levels are so dangerous, operators control the reaction from a separate building. But workers do sometimes handle radioactive material, such as used fuel rods. They must wear protective body suits like this one to limit the risk.

Breathe in
Because the suit must be airtight, an oxygen pack gives fresh air.

Inner wall
The immensely strong inner wall is made of toughened concrete 1.3 m (4 ft) thick. To stop any dangerous gases escaping from the building, it is lined with a tight steel skin.

Roman dome

The ancient Romans built domes to cover a large area with a strong roof, without supporting pillars. Their biggest dome tops the Pantheon, a temple in Rome. Its diameter is about the same as that of the Sizewell B containment building.

Containment building

At 64 m (210 ft) tall and 45.7 m (150 ft) in diameter, the massive containment building houses and protects the parts of the reactor: the pressure vessel, four steam generators, a coolant pump to circulate water round the core, and a pressuriser to keep this water under pressure. To give it strength, the building is made of a double layer of specially reinforced concrete wrapped round a tough framework of steel. Thick concrete also lines the base of the building and surrounds the pressure vessel.

Moving platform
This maintenance platform is mounted on wheels so that it can roll back and forth along the crane.

Maintenance crane
A crane stretches across the containment building, allowing access to the equipment below.

Fuel assembly

The fuel that powers the nuclear reaction is held inside tall towers called fuel assemblies. Each contains 264 fuel rods, metal tubes filled with stacked pellets of radioactive uranium. These are lined up in rows with special control rods between them. When they are lowered towards the fuel rods, the reaction slows down; when they are lifted away, the reaction speeds up again.

Control cluster
The control rods are clustered together to make them easier to lift and lower.

Huge steel frames hold the rods in place

Fuel rods

Control rods

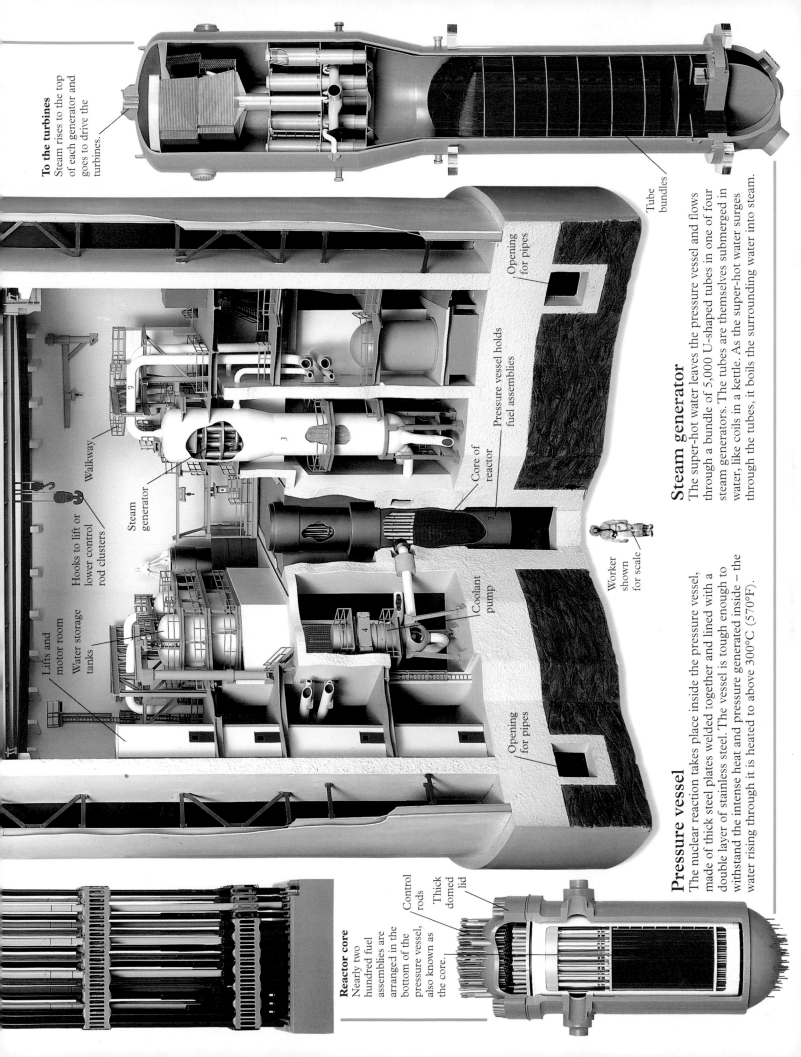

To the turbines
Steam rises to the top of each generator and goes to drive the turbines.

Tube bundles

Steam generator

The super-hot water leaves the pressure vessel and flows through a bundle of 5,000 U-shaped tubes in one of four steam generators. The tubes are themselves submerged in water, like coils in a kettle. As the super-hot water surges through the tubes, it boils the surrounding water into steam.

Opening for pipes

Pressure vessel holds fuel assemblies

Core of reactor

Coolant pump

Worker shown for scale

Opening for pipes

Pressure vessel

The nuclear reaction takes place inside the pressure vessel, made of thick steel plates welded together and lined with a double layer of stainless steel. The vessel is tough enough to withstand the intense heat and pressure generated inside – the water rising through it is heated to above 300°C (570°F).

Walkway

Hooks to lift or lower control rod clusters

Steam generator

Lifts and motor room

Water storage tanks

Reactor core
Nearly two hundred fuel assemblies are arranged in the bottom of the pressure vessel, also known as the core.

Control rods

Thick domed lid

Seabed city

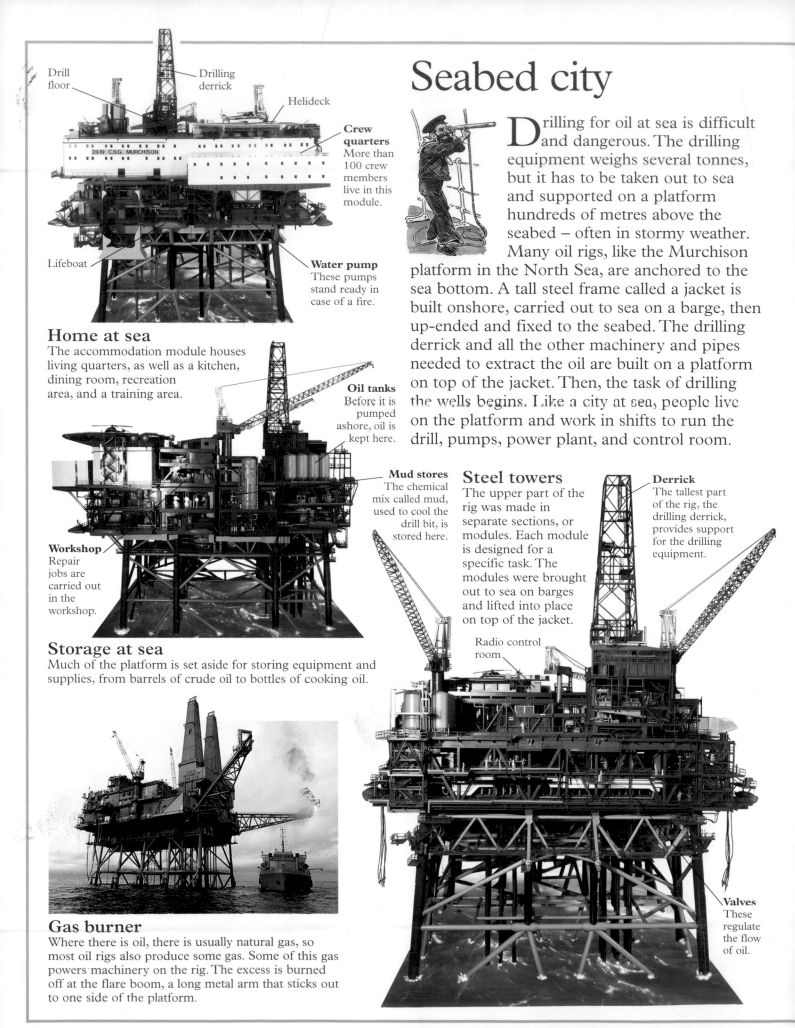

Drill floor

Drilling derrick

Helideck

Crew quarters More than 100 crew members live in this module.

211/19 C.B.G. MURCHISON

Lifeboat

Water pump These pumps stand ready in case of a fire.

Home at sea
The accommodation module houses living quarters, as well as a kitchen, dining room, recreation area, and a training area.

Oil tanks Before it is pumped ashore, oil is kept here.

Workshop Repair jobs are carried out in the workshop.

Mud stores The chemical mix called mud, used to cool the drill bit, is stored here.

Storage at sea
Much of the platform is set aside for storing equipment and supplies, from barrels of crude oil to bottles of cooking oil.

Gas burner
Where there is oil, there is usually natural gas, so most oil rigs also produce some gas. Some of this gas powers machinery on the rig. The excess is burned off at the flare boom, a long metal arm that sticks out to one side of the platform.

Drilling for oil at sea is difficult and dangerous. The drilling equipment weighs several tonnes, but it has to be taken out to sea and supported on a platform hundreds of metres above the seabed – often in stormy weather. Many oil rigs, like the Murchison platform in the North Sea, are anchored to the sea bottom. A tall steel frame called a jacket is built onshore, carried out to sea on a barge, then up-ended and fixed to the seabed. The drilling derrick and all the other machinery and pipes needed to extract the oil are built on a platform on top of the jacket. Then, the task of drilling the wells begins. Like a city at sea, people live on the platform and work in shifts to run the drill, pumps, power plant, and control room.

Steel towers
The upper part of the rig was made in separate sections, or modules. Each module is designed for a specific task. The modules were brought out to sea on barges and lifted into place on top of the jacket.

Derrick The tallest part of the rig, the drilling derrick, provides support for the drilling equipment.

Radio control room

Valves These regulate the flow of oil.

Tower of strength
The derrick supports the weight of the drill string, a long length of heavy pipe attached to the drill bit.

Sea monster
Oil rigs like this one are the world's largest sea-based structures. Its jacket alone weighs more than 25,000 tonnes. The whole platform weighs 48,000 tonnes and is 264 m (866 ft) high. At peak capacity it pumps up some 120,000 barrels of oil a day.

Drilling head
The rig's motor turns a metal platform called a rotary table. This turns the drill string. As the string rotates, the teeth on the drill bit also turn. The weight of the string adds to the force of the drill as it rips through the layers of rock until it strikes oil.

Crane
This is used to unload bulky or heavy objects brought to the rig by supply ships.

Bringing in supplies
An offshore rig may be miles from the mainland, so all supplies have to be brought in specially. Most supplies arrive by ship, but in stormy weather, the helicopter provides the only safe method of transport.

Drill floor
Here beneath the derrick are the pipes and valves that regulate the incoming flow of oil from the producing wells.

Generators
The rig must generate its own power, for everything from pumping oil ashore to heating crew quarters.

Racks for storing extra pipe lengths

Helideck
Helicopters land here to bring supplies and workers to the rig.

Wells
The rig has 24 wells: 12 bring oil to the surface, 10 inject water into the rock, and two are for gas injection.

Jacket
This steel framework supporting the rig extends some 156 m (512 ft) beneath the sea.

Launch pad
A large helideck enables all sizes of helicopter to take off and land in emergencies.

Crane for lifting heavy machinery

Air-filled pontoon

Wire rope anchors on seabed

Keeping afloat
The service vessel is semi-submersible – it floats above the water on round, air-filled "feet" called pontoons. The massive columns that support the decks rise from a pair of pontoons. The vessel is powered by nine enormous diesel engines. When it arrives at the rig, it is moored in position using up to eight anchors on tough wire ropes.

Service at sea

When a building needs repairs, it is usually easy to get to the part that needs fixing. Cranes, scaffolding, and cradles suspended from the roof take painters, maintenance workers, and even window cleaners where they need to go. If there is a fire, fire engines with ladders and booms provide quick access. But what happens with a vast oil rig anchored to the seabed? Some of the work has to be done underwater; other jobs are carried out high up on the rig, often in howling gales. This purpose-built service vessel, used both for underwater and topside operations, provides the ultimate in service at sea. Like a huge floating repair shop, it helps with all the operations required on a rig, from routine inspection and basic repairs, to fighting fires and coping with blowouts and other emergencies.

Control room
A wall of windows all round gives the control room crew a view across a wide area.

Access tower
To reach different parts of the rig, the tower can turn horizontally through a wide angle of 135 degrees.

Tower provides emergency escape route

Signal flags

Crane hook

Triple decker
The two lower decks of the vessel provide enough accommodation for 128 people, from rig maintenance workers and safety inspectors to firefighters and deep-sea divers.

Sprinklers
Rows of water sprinklers for firefighting line the decks of the vessel.

Line represents sea surface

Emergency access
A large 37-m (121-ft) long access tower can swing out over the top of an oil rig. This enables firefighting teams to get on to the rig quickly – and the crew to get off the rig quickly in an emergency.

Dock for submersible

Submersible is docked beneath the service vessel

Submersible
Some parts of an oil rig stretch down hundreds of metres to the seabed. People protected only by diving suits cannot go this deep, so a special submersible is used for deep diving.

Fire practice

One of the most crucial tasks of the service vessel is to bring firefighters and their equipment to a rig. Emergency drills like this one keep the firefighting team in practice.

Jets in action

If there is a fire or blowout (when a drill bit hits a pocket of pressurized oil or gas) on an oil rig, the service vessel saturates the well head with water. It sprays from 16 jets called fire monitors mounted on its decks, delivering up to 151,414 litres (33,311 galls) of water per minute.

Divers at work

Much of the inspection and routine maintenance of an oil rig's supporting jacket is done by divers. This diver wears a special helmet that gives protection from pressure and ocean currents.

Observation tower
This tower supports an observation post as well as communication equipment.

Helicopter on helipad

Load lifter
The crane with the shorter jib can lift weights of up to 50 tonnes.

Access to helipad

Support pillars
The enormous pillars that hold up the decks are made of timber-clad steel.

Propeller
Six propellers help to power the vessel.

All-purpose platform

Although it is well-equipped for emergencies, the service vessel is mostly used for routine work. Its three cranes can load heavy items on to a rig, while its diving facilities are invaluable for joining the under-sea pipelines that connect rigs to the shore.

Pontoon
Rounded metal pontoons keep the vessel afloat.

Glossary

A

Aerodynamic Term used to describe a structure designed so that air will pass over it with minimal resistance, so reducing wind load on the structure.

Aerofoil Structure designed in a similar way to the cross-section of an aeroplane wing.

Pont de Normandie, France

Archaeology The study of the material remains of past human cultures.

Architecture The art and science of designing buildings and supervising their construction.

Atrium Tall internal space in a building, with a glazed roof to let in natural light.

Submersible housed under oil platform

B

Ballast Material used to weigh a structure down, preventing uplift due to wind or water pressure.

Boring machine Mechanism used to excavate a tunnel or other underground structure; often called a tunnel boring machine (TBM).

C

Cable sheaths Protective covering surrounding cables on a bridge.

Cantilever bridge Type of bridge in which fixed arms stretch outwards from anchored piers to support a central span.

Centripetal force Force that acts inwards on a body travelling along a curved path.

Cladding Weatherproof "skin" covering the outside walls of a building.

Cofferdam Structure made of sheet piles or similar elements, designed to keep water out of foundations of such structures as bridge piers.

Computer-aided design The use of computers in the design of buildings and other structures; often abbreviated as CAD.

Cross braces Diagonal members inserted in a rectangular frame to make it more rigid.

Fuel assembly of a nuclear reactor

D

Damper cable Cable fitted between parts of a cable-stayed bridge to reduce vibration.

Deck The floor of a bridge, running between the piers and carrying the roadway or railway line.

Derrick Tower-like framework over an oil well that allows drill tubes to be lowered and lifted.

Drill string Pipe that stretches down from an oil rig to the oil-bearing rock below; oil flows up the pipe and the lower end holds the drill bit.

Duct Channel or tube designed to contain wiring or other services, or to allow air or fluids to flow through.

E

Engineering The profession of applying scientific principles to the design and construction of buildings and structures.

F

Fibre optic cable Cable made of very thin flexible fibres of glass, used to transmit data.

Fly tower Tall structure above the stage of a theatre, enabling scenery and other items to be lowered (or "flown") on to the stage.

G

Gantry A kind of framework used to support a moving overhead crane or similar mechanism.

Triple-looped roller coaster

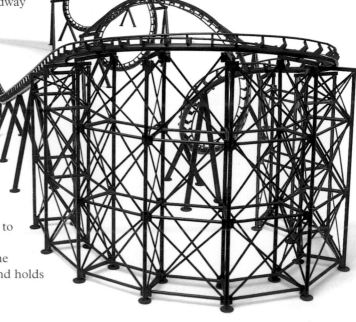

Maintenance crane on top of a skyscraper

Generator
Device used to convert mechanical energy into electricity.

J

Jack Device for raising a heavy object such as a motor vehicle or part of a building.

Jacket Framework that supports an oil rig on the sea bed.

Worker inside service tunnel

M

Maintenance The routine tasks, such as cleaning, painting, and replacing worn parts, needed to keep a structure in a good condition.

Mobile crane Crane that can be moved along a track or on a lorry to the required position.

P

Pier Short wall designed to bear a heavy load such as an arch.

Pillar An upright structure of stone, brick, or metal that holds up part of a building or other structure.

Pontoon Watertight float supporting an oil-rig service vessel, temporary bridge, or similar structure.

Prefabricated Term used to describe parts of a structure that are manufactured off-site and moved to the building site, where they can be assembled quickly.

Pylon Tall, upright structure, to which the cables on a cable-stayed bridge are attached.

R

Reactor Short for nuclear reactor; the incredibly strong container in which the chemical reaction in a nuclear power station takes place.

Reinforced concrete A type of specially strengthened concrete, with steel bars or mesh embedded inside it.

S

Sill Horizontal ledge below a window; or, the lowest horizontal part of a frame.

Skyscraper Tall, multi-storey building, the weight of which is supported by a metal framework.

Span Distance between the supports of a bridge or arch.

Spoil Rock and other waste material dug up in an excavation.

Structure Name for any complex construction.

Suspension bridge Bridge in which the deck is hung from ropes or cables passing over twin towers.

T

Terminal In an airport, a purpose-built building for arrivals and departures.

Topside Upper part of an oil rig or service vessel, above the water level.

Truss Structural framework used to support a roof or bridge.

Eurostar car-carrying wagon

Turbine Machine with a bladed rotor that turns to convert the energy of a moving fluid into mechanical energy.

V

Valve Device that turns on or off, or controls, the flow of a liquid or gas.

Ventilation System that provides control over the air quality in a building, by removing stale air and allowing fresh air to come in.

Viaduct Bridge with many spans carrying a road or railway, often across a valley.

W

Welding Attaching two pieces of metal or plastic by softening them with heat.

Reactor pressure vessel

Index

Acknowledgements

Design assistance:
Rachael Dyson, Iain Morris, Emma
Bowden, Salesh Patel, and Jason
Gonsalves

Photoshop retouching:
Bob Warner

Illustrations:
John Woodcock

Thanks to:
Gary Ombler for photographic
assistance, Nicky Studdart for DTP
design, Nicola Waine for editorial
assistance, Neville Graham for design
guidance in the early stages of the book,
and Marion Dent for the index.

Dorling Kindersley would also like to
thank Donald and Arthur Smith of
Donald Smith Modelmakers for their
kind permission to photograph their
model of the service vessel and the oil

platform, the Aberdeen Maritime
Museum, the staff of the Thames Barrier
Visitor's Centre, the staff of the Sizewell
B Press Office, Katy Harris of Sir
Norman Foster and Partners, Sylvia
Jones at the Eurotunnel Exhibition
Centre, John Staunton and John Loader
at Ove Arup and Partners, Robert
Marshall at Barton Myers Associates,
Roderick Coyne and Francis Graves at
Alsop & Störmer Architects, M. Nicolas
Fritz of the Department of Architecture
and Building in Marseille, Clare Endicott
at Michael Hopkins & Partners, Chigusa
Oshima at Kansai International Airport
Co, Ltd, and Shunji Ishida and Isabella
Carpiceci at the Renzo Piano Building
Workshop.

Picture credits
r=right, l=left, t=top, c=centre, b=below,
a=above.

Alsop and Störmer: 16tr, 17tl, 17tr;
Ancient Art and Architecture: 18tr;
British Gas Plc: 19tr; **Mary Evans
Picture Library:** 10cr, 11r, 20cr, 24cr,
30tr, 34tr, 36tr; **Sir Norman Foster
and Partners:** 10 ar, 10cr, 11cr, 12al;
Dennis Gilbert: 9tl, 32cl, 32c; **Robert
Harding Picture Library:** 20tr, 24tr,
29tr; **Michael Hopkins and Parnters:**
8b, 9tr, 9b; **The Image Bank:** 25c,
Gary Gladstone 35tc; **Kansai
International Airport Co. Ltd.:** 32tr;
Ian Lambot: 12tl, 12br, 12tr, 13l, 13b,
13r; **Frank Lane Picture Agency:**
25c; **Magnum Photos Limited:** 27tr,
Jean Gaumy 27tc; **Barton Myers
Associates:** 14bl, 15tl, 15tr;
Popperfoto: 11c, 28tr, 33cr;

QA Photos Ltd: 20cl, 20c, 22tl,
23br; **Renzo Piano Building
Workshop:** 8cl, 8cr; **Rex Features:**
19cr, 30c, 32cr, 35cl, 38bl, 41tl,
/Berry Bingel 39tr, /Kiry O'Donnel
18tr,/Sipa 30bl, /Sipai/Marais
Gaussen 12cl, /Andrew Testa 31tl,
/The Times 36tr, /Mike Toy 41tr;
Science Photo Library: 36br,
37bc, /Martin Bond 25cl, /Richard
Folwell 41tc, /David Parker 8cr;
Thames Barrier: 29tl; **Thames
Water Utilities Limited:** 18bl,18c;
Unichrome Bath Limited: 29br;
Zefa Pictures: 39tc

Every effort has been made to trace
the copyright holders. Dorling
Kindersley apologises for any
unintentional omissions and would
be pleased, in such cases, to add an
acknowledgement in future editions.